By the Bias of Sound
Selected Poems:
1974 – 1994

By the Bias of Sound
Selected Poems:
1974 – 1994

Gustaf Sobin

Talisman House, Publishers
Jersey City, New Jersey

Published by Talisman House, Publishers
129 Wayne Street
Jersey City, New Jersey 07302

Selections from Gustaf Sobin, *Wind Chrysalid's Rattle*
and *Celebration of the Sound Through*,
copyright © 1980, 1981, 1982 by Gustaf Sobin.
Used by permission of The Montemora Foundation, Inc.

Selections from Gustaf Sobin, *The Earth as Air*,
Voyaging Portraits, and *Breath's Burials*,
copyright © 1984, 1988, 1995 by Gustaf Sobin.
Used by permission of New Directions Publishing Corporation.

Library of Congress Cataloging-in-Publication Data

Sobin, Gustaf.
    By the bias of sound : selected poems, 1974-1994 / Gustaf Sobin.
        p.   cm.
    ISBN 1-883689-21-X (cloth). – ISBN 1-883689-20-1 (paper)
    I. Title
    PS3569.037B9   1995
    811'.54–dc20   95-13274
                                                                        CIP

for SUSANNA

CONTENTS

from
WIND CHRYSALID'S RATTLE
(1974)

•

from
CELEBRATION OF THE SOUND THROUGH
(1980)

•

•

The dates given for the various books
correspond to the dates of their creation,
not their publication.

By the Bias of Sound
Selected Poems:
1974 – 1994

from
WIND CHRYSALID'S RATTLE
(1974)

. . . everything has been given to human-
kind from the very beginning but as a
portable quantity that they might carry
with them —throughout their entire jour-
ney— the totality of whatever need be
created.

Lucien Sebag

SIGNS

what matters   is what the shadow   says:
        is reading the cloud, and the   spastic drift
of dragonflies
    over the glass-headed meadow.

is earth, its ciphers.   its membrane   of sounds.
    is one's life   risked, a miracle
                        within a lizard's eyes!

isn't
that's almost (its vastness, infinitesimal: a glint
  in the voice's wondrous shadows). *isn't*

that dreams   itself: the translucent herd of its
  kisses driven, ineluctable, the

earth germinal driven   into the absence that *is.*

THAT THE UNIVERSE IS CHRYSALID
(Blake's Birthday)

that the universe is chrysalid.

that all things that are, are continuous emanations.

that their being is a perpetual becoming.

that becoming is the breath of lust. and that lust is perfection.

that all increments are equal.

the spore is the clavicord of the tree.

the clavicord is lust.

that in creating we extend the very energy that's created us.

that this extension is space.

that space, the space we move through, and dwell in, is made up
of the infinitesimal crystals that we murmur.

music hears.

that creation is momentum made perceptible.

the attempt to store or isolate momentum is tyranny.

not sequence, but elaboration.

that genesis is a wind.

the rock ripples; the night swims.

that the eyes are forever swifter than their green mirrors.

that structure is shadow.

that music should catch fire and flame into gesture, motion,
deed.

that the past hasn't yet happened.

that only the edge is dominion. only the edge secretes.

that our lust is lightness. acceleration.

and what we call the 'stillness' is the inconceivable velocity of our
flesh, thinking in the same space-cadence as the universe.

the thrust of a single whisper.

the lymph, the lightning!

that life, in its ecstatic throes, touches the resplendence of death.

that the senses shall iridesce into their infinite sensations.

that we become, ultimately, the space we've created.

~

blossoming generatrix, and genius of our every breath.

HELIX

liquid, the dawn's
green axe.

the sheer agility of wrists,
calves,
of the eyes swimming
into the earth's
first clouds.

why wait?
what holds?
the breath sprouts,
sprouts flutes,
the horn's spiralling glass.

villages rise
in wheels of rich dust,
while a creature
begs for herself,
buoyed
in the glittering arms of her voice.

HELIX

dawn
diamonds the wind.

alive.
alive,
and risking ourselves
on reaching
the inevitable.

thighs, boulders, lightning,
we're deep pods
of breath
breathing ourselves
into light.

my teeth; your shoulders.

flesh
in the throe of its flower,
the air's
spiralling meadow's,
our radiance
is what the wind-crystals sing,
and the black earth
echoes.

ALL OCTAVES SIMULTANEOUS
for Rhiannon

saw earth as eventual.

saw each thing in its dumb, ecstatic solitude.

cold dawn. swift wrists.

out of an underworld came, carrying her lantern of burning
seeds.

word's germinal spin: its helix.

billow the arms, the hair, out of the breathing words.

speak until the lizard sings. until the wind's dagger glows.

breath-of-life as language.

as the eye opens, the star grows; as the tongue touches, the flesh
blooms.

a form forever wider than the widening dissolutions.

shook the wind free of its red shrubs.

detaching, gathered.

only elation, in its cryptic waves, is coalescence, is wisdom.

became the other the instant morning became me.

all the glassy fruit, wrestling free.

blow out of the oboes of genesis, the shivering ions.

live the length, the thirst of this white vibration.

larks, through the siphon of their voices, soar.

the soil searches for the eye of the searching root.

perspective, in its cubes, the length of its verb, will collapse, at last, into its deepest orchard.

not writing, but waiting; waiting for the recurrent miracle: the breath in the eclipse of its bones.

was at the earth's edge, gathering sound.

lay, feeling the entire length of the wind, its iridescence, within me.

suffered the bliss of each finger.

in the long hesitation of a rock, watched its slow tendons meditate.

creation risks itself on a harp of red clay.

in the midst of voluptuous space, a metaphor has encaged us.

crouched for the immaculate leap.

the magpies scatter the sun. feed it on dragonflies.

the dreams were real: were viscous windows looking out onto ourselves who were already other.

was looking for their voices (where I'd found, in a pear orchard,
a circle of flint tools).

feeling the emptiness, I gave it its name. repeated its syllables,
over and over, until it formed, in successive tissues, a sphere, a
sound-sculpture, standing within the vacated air.

not the things, but the blissful filament that runs, oscillating,
through them.

our least words *walk* in one another's dreams.

wind, whose iris we are. whose stutter.

what you say, said the voice with the green, momentary eyes of
an oak, is what you hear: hear me saying.

scribbled, and a wall of light, furiously vertical, rose.

had begun equalling ourselves: begun dying into our own incon-
ceivable beauty.

each word is already *edged* with new earth.

off the breath's blue spools unravel the planets.

the mud guttural, the mosses whistling, where a single step, the
boot's bristling crystals, crams the universe.

the earth-rock still reverberating in the axe, held upright in the
dark air.

deep down, the kisses dream.

the ring of the lamp is forever wider than its reflections.

the eyes, clamped shut, squeeze to a star.

the lover is the beauty of the beloved.

we're alive between two echoing boulders of vast blackness.

this is, that wasn't: a sprinkling of words in the wind's humus.

the future forever *returns*.

ends in inception: a grief spawning its small fist of white shadow.

so dark only the light was visible.

pollen is its own godhead.

HELIX

the mist burns
to a bronze whisper.

fields
are the dense, inverted
facets
of a glaucous star.

I taste
and exhale them.

wind's skin,
where space,
into its chrysalid, contracts.

amongst
its breathing minerals
I recognize
my mirror.

lip,
lips,
and the blind spine's
bright
shiver.

EFFIGY: ULTIMATELY, THE SISTER

forced beyond   me (through
                        the   illegible light);
forced to   find: to   imagine the
     image
that might   imagine me;
that might,
     replying (in   degrees
                        of increasing   density),
     restitute and

     return me.

                    ~

     return, and   rename me.

     for what I am
     would be made out   of castings, of
each word's
     inversion,
               as a breath
beating against the air's   bright metal
     would make of it   its effigy.

                    ~

effigy.   the burning surfaces
               at each instant's   extremity.

               the echo-sheets.

     for even the infinite
would crease, and the infabled bodies   touch,
     touch, and   rubbing,
                    mould themselves,

invent themselves
in the wet   wavering mirrors of   the other.

~

    the path
would ride backwards, and the   least stones
            star and   interpret me.
    the hills, within, and the hidden trees
would issue,   surrounding me in   the ring
                of their   fresh releases.

    pure twin
    of contrariety. dark sister
    in the still drifting chrysalis of sleep,
the image,
the beautiful limbs of the unbidden   image,
    blown through, and   beyond me,
would resound. and my   voice, refracted,
would at last   reply,

    touched by its own   incestuous sounds.

MAKING THE MIRROR

mirror, my first light, my darkest mineral.

nothing I say, but that I'm said; nothing I touch, but that I'm touched.

for each thing: its breathed equivalent: its spatial counterweight.

the tongue-cast anatomy of the other: the errant twin.

no way of seeing you without astonishing myself.

presence is tension: tension with an absence that, elsewhere, is equally present.

for the archer, only the interval is sacred.

it's the breath-crystals alighting that constitute the mirror.

we were not meant to be saved, but to seize and be seized by intense identities.

writing: to temper myself against a surface of living replies.

nothing in the thing, but the thing reflexive: in its own dialectical echo.

bend the flaccid glass of the light. make it your bow.

it's the beloved, within us, that becomes the poem.

perilous throne of a voice. its voices.

the mirror, vanishing; its fugitive reflections.

age of eaten effigy.

a path is gasping at a cloud.

a land has elapsed, unfabled, unhappened.

five days in the imageless city — blazing heart!

pain answers pain; makes a luminous appeal to power.

the minuscule, utterly magical cleavage within the body.

to split the instant and create an interlude, a moment of historic
evasion into which our entire life could rush.

luminous chairs!

to feel, finally, the tree, touching my finger.

it's by what we didn't see that we'll recognize ourselves.

spread hands glorying against the gushing source.

the force flowing against us is also ours.

PORCELAIN

enough
of each of us   isn't
to beg of the   other: our   echoing whiteness;

to see, through the bunched   iris, beyond us,
our fluid   star (grown   even whiter)

floating against the   wind-walls of the light.

BOTH

pulls light out of   stone.
pulls   smoke that ripples like   skins,
gildings over the   eyes,

that warps
the minutes,
makes love to the dark   heart that delivers it.

HELIX

wasp
autumn.
the gold's
rotting
in the long winds;
the tips of the fingers fume.

who'll know
the orbits
of the new hours,
the brown-haired wheels
of their hymns?

the grape-
crates thunder.
and through the weather's
ear
the root
transluces.

our faces
fuse.
the vines
ignite.

into
a bloom
of intricate feathers
the full dusk
blazes.

1

wanting to say   what I'd hear,
wanting to say
      what it is that   I wanted to hear,

(while moving, wordless, through the   white
    weightless shell,

                reading shadows,

                nudging rocks).

~

wanting to say:
wanting to   hear
      what it is that   I wanted to say.

since hearing
    was what I was,
    was what it was that   enveloped me
        in the ear   of an enveloping ellipse.
    what held me
    while   space
chanted   wheeling through the   black chambers
of each cell,
      and heard itself   heard in

      the hearing I was,

      as I was the   space,
      as I was what   it was I heard.

~

words
aren't enough; are the attempt at words;
are what words, generating themselves,

                                        would say.

but saying, first, is   reaching;   is reclaiming
        the breath
        that the breath   cleaved; its
                                ruptured expanse:
        its land
of doubles, of dissolving   echoes,
where the circles
        search for their   edge: rim
where the rock   would quiver,
and each word
        reappear,   ribbed in its magnitude.

                        ~

        for saying, in itself,
        says nothing. saying
is the breath, in the   shred of its syllables,
thrust, projected
        against space's
                        mirrored extremity:
        the tissue of each   breath in its entity.

where
the body, being named,
        would resound,
        would feel itself   slowly enveloped
in the arms and hair,
        in the luminous hands of   its own hearing,

hearing itself   in the same word as its saying;
hearing itself   said
                        in its hearing.

who are you (who was, once,   myself);
who are you
        who'd listen,
        who'd   hear?
(who was, once, the   girl whose   eyes burnt,
      tugging at her scarf of   cerulean stars).

what
would   contain, what membrane   withstand
    this torch of   nerve,
    the blown fibers of   a saying, of   a life
inside the   inflamed tongue
    of a saying,
            that says   nothing.

who are you,
who,   being touched, would touch and
    touching, would withhold the   instant,
    the word in its   infinite accretion,
        would withhold it, and   hear.

        ~

wanting to say,
wanting to say the   eyes
    in which   the eyes would, at last, resound,
    and each limb,
          reflect;
(where
    projection, in its lost orchards, replies).

who are you,
who are you   who's breathing through me?
    whose hair   braids itself in   my breath?
who still   wordless
is waiting in   shimmers

for your name to   name me,
and to wrap yourself,
a new   creature, in the   flesh of   your mirrors.

from
CELEBRATION OF THE SOUND THROUGH
(1980)

rides the line of myself outwards (the

measure) to a
first ripple's

return.

---

reduces air
to
this handful of
sounds,
thrives
vibrant inside it,
survives
the
white
wind-flaked
relic, be-
yond.

. . . .dark
for the long eyes
drawing
their chalk
through.

all summer
emptied the
hills (as if
something
less than my
hands
would
reach you).

you never knew
you
were me;
you

never were.   walked in
and out
of your own
inappeasable
eye; weren't

even
you.

was no
room white
enough to
catch
this:
this
lightning,
your
fabulous
lash.

---

it came up, off
your face, filled
everything.

---

the quick
of the wind: the wind's
gold isn't
what we
thought, is
exactly what
we've never
thought, is
why the ruins in
the high hills
crouch so
in-
side it.

myself:
my
eyes-in-leaves, keeping

the mind
mindless,
alert,
away from the
hive
where the
halves

might
touch.

---

coming
down
even brighter.   light rising
from
each finger, over
the eyes, out
onto the

slope.

---

an alphabet
of glass
let-
ting what it
says (its
clay
instants)
come
through.

---

quicker: that
nothing
be lost (that al-
ready in
the gray surf, be-
yond our own eyes'
evasions,
we
could catch glimpses
of ourselves).

---

white waves
moving
over black (bone-

lines
of the mind).

---

as if
a
sacrifice in
the name
of the
null, that

swollen
light, its
liquidity,

sent
across.

———————————————

no way
away
from

me, other
than

you, you
moving
out-

side your-
self, be-

yond
your white

replies.

WHERE

only words   could
catch   words: keep them (our-
selves inside   them) from the flagellant whir,

from being wingbeaten into the   else,
the ever-
        extracting where.

voice
that the voices
couldn't feed on.   the iris
of the wine
wrinkling
in a

tall breeze, the
terraces
pressed through the lids . . .
love,

this swollen lamp
you've
dressed in
has deepened.   a

myrrh
of nerves
curls through the tendons:
trellises.
trap

of octaves!   whispers
beating
against bone!   a breath-

threading breath
through all the
amber that
pours
over the long-winged boulders.

ODE

for Charles Tomlinson

1

were saying these things to   stop them,

to   keep them   from
being said by   the ceaseless (the un-

sayable).

~

held,   holding them: the breath's gold:
Rembrandt's

black
elephants.   because luminous   is
what we've learnt to   darken   (to
circumscribe) with   sound: hoop
to this
circus
of   inversions.

~

images.   tokens and
images:

all   we know; that we'll ever   know of
ourselves.   im-
prints of an
obliterating
as-

cendency (fingers
poking
over the coils of the   fuming kelp).

~

what
we call holiest
goes under.   whatever's
ours is

only ours
against.

in crypts
of whispers,
mud-
hovels, our white   chords
hoarded; all
our bright-winged
demons

ballasted
in   blood.

2

all   we know; that we'll ever know . . . .

but the flare, the
clamoring
flue of
the
limbs, up-
wards . . . . lovelier
than anything
we've   ever known.   the lessening

into immensity.   the spreading   trees
of the instants
in bud.   each worded   circle, re-

lapsing, trans-
lucent, into the   eye-
alleviant
of   loss.

~

we'll never   say
what we'd   say.   the jealous   soil, its
syntax,
keeps us doubled to our-
selves.   a voice-net

shrivels us
in its   chimeras.

but the sense,
forever,
swells outwards.   the null,
sumptuous, draws   at the divided voice.

hear the
intervals
as they pour through the   comb of their
octaves; and the   words,
boned
of   all but their   breath,
spread
radiant.

~

was why
he   turned.   why

startled, out-
raged, she stopped. and felt her   rip-
pling tall-hipped body
dissolve
to a
word.

wings.

wings!   all we have   instead of   wings!

PHRASINGS

pure wound, the white   earth earlier, e-
qual.   its hills
                   no   higher than its meadows.

---

        the bees   locked
in all that wisteria, the   cool fume of its

   cones   (hallucinatory dungeon).

---

        later
came the first   mirrors: the frail   breath-
combs.

---

everything said: said in-   stead of.

---

puz-
zling thunder.   o-
pen

vocable.

———————————————

there's that.   only
that, and it's   nothing, you say, squint-
     ing into it,   nothing,
nothing at   all.

———————————————

turning the twig of a   word: releasing its

silences.

———————————————

the Things,
the   Things, in be-
     tween the words, ex-   ist.   peer through.

---

the locked bodies nighted, *neithered* to
themselves.

---

it's the eye that sculpts the apple, feasts

on its white peelings.

---

tense projections: at each instant: retractable.

---

only this   hand to
hold you, its un-
ringed fingers, letting go.

---

even here at the   very
edge, even   this to be opened,   emptied,
chanted free
of it-
self.

———————————————

depth, the

mouth (the unsoundable   island).

———————————————

to chase your   name
        down into   darkness: to   capture its

amnestic glints.

CÀ D'ORO

bulbed
out-
wards, the
imbarcadero
len-

ses the
senses.   water-
cut, the words
slip

through.   your
world, in those
immense

muscles of
hair, the lime-
green linens
you travelled with.
once

still is.   the
heavens

unravelled.   on a
wrist,

over the taut
rocked water, the
white barge

pivots.

are given the distances, the tenses: toward.

to move through everything you'd ever let go of.

flowering masks!

were worshipping the word you couldn't interpret.

wild, luminous, serene: that eye that's blowing through you.

. . . through the breezeroots.

'nothing' was never 'no one.'

were: what you moved towards against your own oncoming re-
plies.

lavish eliminator: liminal Eve.

through the sparkling wastes, those lupine angels, extending the
scaffolds of space.

chasm-weeds.

a heart, honking at nothing, treading air, guessing at itself.

was still what you didn't know to guide you: its light, like a lumi-
nous clay, to unearth.

why the dragonflies moored, immobile, over the drifting instant.

leasting air to those sudden beads.

letting the words take you towards wherever they'd come from.

a mouth: for rooting in.

what pulled you toward it, and touched, like an iris, only itself.

. . . had a name; had only a name.

sperm-let, that it couldn't be told, but continuously shuttle, like a blank money, a frenetic stillness.

were setting yourself to sound.

scaled heart!

wedging the air to its white alphabets.

to sleep in the face you'd never reach: the light of the face you'll never return from.

~

up through their
gray   oily torsos (in weight-
less waterfalls of   light) is earth-the-word
that's lifting, re-
leasing the   earth, letting

it out.

~

the eye, by
itself, would go on   and on.   but *there*, the
flying meat, in those   sudden
vermilion instants, shatters and   replies. . . .

(like the petals, blown
in out of   where you'd been moving towards).

~

wasp-hearted, their bracelets
of cold coral-   white blossoms, are what
you'd written: that   heap

of shadows you're   telling yourself to. . . .

~

a madrigal
of   branches.   off the lowest (flowing
    ruffled, like   a chopped current) the
badger
will be feeding—lunarian—on the pigeon's heart.

~

only *visible* to yourself in the instant that
that phosphor   vanishes (through the
   tendons of   the cherry: the quills, in the
wake   of the quills, alive in   their annihilating
                        updraft).

~

luenh es lo castelhs

like threads the
petals, in the lee of   the deep ruts, run
        on and   on. . . . . 'never'

was what those wind-   broken jugglers meant.

1

spoke, but couldn't
say (what
it was, sound's

empty
yet preponderant thing:
as if

to stand here, in near-
spring, before the
first

squirting vineshoots, the
earth, still a death-
hoof, a no-

head, to say 'me,' to
be depended on
the clatter

of those dry un-
substantiated syllables.
look, here's a

leaf, and
there: there's another . . .
'leaf' breaks—as

I say it—volatilized
between the lips
and teeth).

o all
that insistence, that ganging
of stars in-

to a single in-
voluted syntax; such
densities, for

circumscribing what?—a
breath? *'per-
mettez-moi d'ex-*

primer cette apprehension,
demeure
une incertitude. . . .'

'compose.   (no ideas
but in. . . .)'
grammatik.

floats, im-
mobile, in the frieze
of its

ribboning woodsmoke. . .
the village, the
image, the al-

ways *else*
that tells us, tell
us: 'we're here.'   but

the reflection
we've made and pro-
jected about us, like

some cylinder of
light, is
riddled.   substance

flees.   and through
the breath-
invested intervals, its

blown threads
flare. . . . is ours, what
isn't, what

we've
worked free of the
'here,' and its echoing-

rhetorical 'there.'   are
neither's, the
no-

where's, but this
bright draft
between.

4

'through,'
not 'towards,' was
the word that

took me—each
time—past
myself, and into the

null's
suspended accelerant.
(were others I

knew
who'd twisted wings
out of rags

and arm-
lengths of wire; while
still others, the loveliest,

turned and
turned, and even
in their braided dreams, only

saw blue).

Envoy

'I,' word
that I come upon, happen
in, in this

wind-
beater's language, the
mirror-syllable, *am*

these things
that I've teased forth
into translucence: the sheer

tooth and flower, at
earth's end, the very earth
yet to appear.

TROUBADOUR

what I love's the
squander, to
spend
and spend, through the
cold air 'run

with the pennants,' as if
world

were still
to be reached, wrung from its
mirrors: wind, gypsum,
brushweed,
all

those des-
olate metals.   its
meanings
breached, blown

through. you'd
turned

to a distance.   with-
in you (the skirt, the
pearl of
your skirt spreading, like a *resonance*,
an *element*) I'd risen.
routes

of Provence, smoke
in drafts through the black cypresses. . .
'there's this, this,' you
tell me.   as the

fingers open, they're
filling
with curls.

. . . chewed
on that
rippling

gold; threaded
it, wet,
to a

tautness.   so
huge
with un-

doings, our
lives (are
what

we'd quickened
into
still-

ness. . . . . had
driven, our
chins

wedged, into
that deep
leaf-

less dark
we're
strung to. . . . .

. . . .
. . . .
. . . .)

lay
there, in a
wave of

white
angles, while
the mirrors

blew
out, over
us, like eyelids.

the shadow, within, thinks of itself as substance
   while what it   wishes (the other)
appears as   substance, is only
                        its obliterating reply.

----

         if the shadow points
it's because the   shadow's drawn; drawn, I
      call it 'you,' 'yours,'
               when it's never yours   but

the glint you make   that pulls the shadow through . . .

. . . all one's darkness being weighed,   risked
            in those   thin
                     tin-   white quivers.

----

you, because
     I didn't want, never asked for myself,
but slaked, each time,
               on your shattered mirrors.

---

under a breeze-cloth of   glances, is letting
              the light bones   go.

---

if word   is, if
     world is, it's outside *what-*

ever it is that wishes to name, number,   elaborate.

---

     is the shadow-
within-the-   flesh, reflected, that permits passage; is
    nothing before or   beyond it, only
               its 'between.'

---

through the narrows   that
        draft of   fumes as it thickens
to a murmur: the white   rhyme of its dissolution. . . .

────────────────

filled the world with   ourselves; then, invented a
        grail, ir-

resonant enough.

────────────────

        the fingers, curling
                into claws, to
withhold the   rolled smoke of the shadows (as if

                        they could).

────────────────

as the fanned lashes   touch, the smoke
                        cones through.

────────────────

on   and on, one soul
         ridding itself upon   another: our heaven-cir-

cuitous.

---

         rushed, each time, towards the
   hollowest, the 'heart   of lepers,' this

                     gift   of our needlessness.

---

awash in those ashes, still talked   of roses. . . . .

---

         am the   transparent mask that
                 you've made: in half-circles, the
   wild ash   rubbed into arms, shoulders, your
                     long   glowing face.

---

to bury our shadows   under the
lashes of
their reflection is what   we mean, murmur of. . . .

THE CHEVAL GLASS
(*T'ang*)

glances back-
wards be-

tween the
two
turquoise flamingoes;
fingers

swim to her cheeks,
fork
through
those tossed fires . . .
my

shadows, too, drift
into the image, my
arms take
root

in her sleeves. . . .
so

many cells for that
gray
glowing oval; her
pearls spill,
clicking,

be-
tween
its tapering beaks.

from
THE EARTH AS AIR
(1982)

MADRIGAL

with you
what I know of

the world
opens, has

that of
swelling, wave as

it tatters, a
ruled line, against

reefs, a
breadth that

still
spreading, breaks

in-
to dull tokens, spent

petals, what the
poem

would
close on, hold

in its
swift tissues, those

blown
ex-

panses,
shadows as

if
pouring, light

from your
fingers, your

blue, un-
loosened sash.

ELEVEN QUATRAINS AND A NOTE
FROM VENTADOUR

    neither this   world's nor
another's, that   broken house with
                 its books and   wind,

bells sewn on the   breathing veils,   between.

----

    with their wire, moon-
        flat baskets, came searching
for the   rain's meat, those
      readers of   ditches, dark   margins.

----

    as if listening, in
        that barge of
blue chalk and   choked linen, to
        her own waves as they   rose . . . .

----

over the fixed smoke
of the almonds, the   other, the
            gypsies' (their rabbits   roasting

            in the wind-
            less light . . . .).

----

            untouched, grown monstrous
with my own shadows, o
                        hooded lilies (the
suns   shimmying upon the skin of   the ditch).

----

            way the eyes   slide, an
                  instant slower than the   face, the
hair lugged —like a trophy— over
                        the shoulders,   after.

----

you only   could
take your gaze from   my keeping (tease it:
        cold, nebulous,   through
        the taut shadows of   your teeth).

---

        the heart forever offered, en-
            trusted to   its own
perditions: that weird   inadmissible rose,
                    valentin froissé.

---

        glances back-
wards through the vaulted loop
        of her arms. rasp,

as the blue   rhinestone hairclips
                    slip under.

in these white shadows, the   wind-
      light we live   in, would perish
without the word-
    pleated waves: that
                  cadence we   give them.

---

    as the petals catch
against the blond   canebreaks: say,
    say nothing; it's enough, if

a wrist went blind on   its own whispers.

---

    always towards the   end, the
grammarians. *albas*, our
    dawn songs: on what terraces,
   onto the carved waters
of what viol
      shall our hearts be   pitched?

GIRANDOLE

1

towards dawn, the
taxis
      idle
before the glass doors . . .
. . . .
fuchsia,

where a blown hem flares
in the sudden
updraft,
then

settles
pearl through
a broken
foam

of reflections.

~

an ankle
arches, as the
mouths open, and fill . . .
a world-

without.
what the instinct
would swell to: that

image, that
deep

ray-
headed mirror
in which the dark breath
un-

wrinkles.

. . . .

wrapt
shadows, swept
fates . . .

                    in the rush,
uptown, the
moon
slips, over and
over, off the polished
wings

of the streaked
fenders.

                    2

it's how the
scarf falls, and
the

soft
braided silver
of the shoes . . . their signs!
that sky! the
new

un-
declinated night!
whisper

chases whisper, edge
its edges,
as

an arm swims
toward the
cast
brass palmleaves
of the light.

~

break, but
where; shatter, a
wave, still
swelling, against what? . . .
. . . .

. . . no
heaven, and
scarce-

ly an
earth, a-
wash in that last echo: a
mouth as it

twists
to the fold of a shoulder.

IRISES
for Susanna

out of those wild, in-
      visible circuits, a
hawkmoth   flew in. was dawn (in
    deep vases, the   first
              white lines of the iris).

----

     way that they ruffle   in
that rock   windcell (that their buds   un-
             scroll and   open: opened,

    asking myself only   for what I see . . . .).

----

    like birds trapped   in
      those tall,   still-
glistening frescoes: the errant   etruscan's.

----

earth it-
self held
in

that silent
ven-
triloquy.

———————————

muscled in
washed golds or
waves   of pale naples, these deep
androgynies: a

joust of buds and   limp
relenting petals.

———————————

my lines, for an instant, become   theirs (but
only
for the   extravagation).

———————————

75

rise, loop-winged, in a   volley
of light yellows, stalks   caught
          in slender   rectangular jars . . . .

being invisible, we
          sip at those   open
emanations: tubers shot into   tall
          grottoes, emptied
                              wind-   eaten tombs.

lovely, the irises in their deep
          oblivion, wounds   open on
what the poem would
          close: catch   in the purities of its fiction.

a surf of
          frozen whites, for   your eyelids; its
waves, that
          pitched linen, for   your sleep . . . .

(*faïence de moustiers*)

    not the javelins stabbing
into their own   azurous mass, but the bowl, the
                    cold, sun-   broken round . . . .

    are corpses, too: the petals   streaming
            against the hard   stalks, or
wizened, sack-
        like, in the tissued shadows   of their wings.

                (*Saint Vincent's*)

    those cold fires on
their piped   stems don't flower, they
                alight, perch there in   pale,
        insane violets . . .

(are prayers, are the smoke   of prayers . . .).

are awe-

weights (for
weighing

a

grief
against . . .).

---

the dead   go on drinking, speckle
the white table   saffron
with their   transparent inks . . . .

---

each iris: the   shell
of an   iris, the papery craters
of its spent
ebullience.

---

mass gutted for the sake of   an inference.

———————————————————

are the lines of   flight of
        these floral   chases (not the
blades, the buds, the skirts   blown, buff-
    white, over the draft of
                        their thighs),

but the lines   driven quilled
        into the drawn lips   of the invisible.

———————————————————

———————————————————

                    (*viaticum*)

    the dried irises in the
        sleeves of the   oil lamps
are yours —for   your journey— for dimming
                    those   gaudy winds with .   .   .

wrapt to the
eyes in
loose, blue hooding, lugged —over the
last rocks— those
threaded
whispers. *Col
de Vallongue*, where the crows
unhook, and the
suns
rise, disheveled, with their winds . . . .

would enter, had
said, slipping
light into
light, wedging dawn
   with those thin, splintered crystals.
in bowls,
the

glowing
crags. currents
that the goshawks, soon, would
take to.

ever the part, un-
worlded. at the errant center, that
locked muscle, the
mirror of
its

own unreflecting
integer . . . .

long straps, slapping,
way
that the path bobbed
against bone. that the scree jingled
with the spill of
its
black, ice-
lacquered blades.

La Caume, in
a drift
of barbed
thistles. *Glanum* greek over *Saint*
Remy. where,
once, the
stars got washed, the
cypresses still rose —swollen— into that in-
voluted
air.

higher, saw
the Rhone dangle, and the
trembling tin
of

its spread
estuary. *Les*
Baux sudden, as if stranded, barge
floating fixed
over the
low, domed groves
of its olives. *Altas*
ondas
que venez suz la mar, sang Vaqueiras, who'd
worn the peacock, known
its pointed
star.

past *le mas de*
Chevrier, a
sputter
of flushed partridge. clouds rising, like
Elijah's, in high,
wind-
piled spirals.

winds;
would learn
the

winds' names; in
oc, the
words for 'moss' and 'mineral' and 'fern.'
for it's
through the words
we'd

enter, would
wed

that overhanging
jelly-
headed light. where path
would turn into pine, and pine into those
flaccid, ice-
green
fires . . . .

towards *le*
Planet
ruts run double, ruler-straight, across
rock. dwarf-
oak and
juniper —as conjugates— dropped
beneath the
last aleppos, to *Saint*

Gabriel. the
plains, at

last, that pampered
ground. terns, working at the wheat's
edge; a canebreak,
a-

flame: smoke,
twisted
through brass. on the
tow-

path, now, towards
Tarascon,
ten steps, exactly, between the squat
platans,
pruned sheer.
the fields, now, as
they break
into gardens, and the ragged
quince-
hedges thicken. the bells, the
dense bells of *Sainte-Marthe* already, and the
black
workshops blue
with their heavy acetylene stars . . . .

would
enter, had said, the breath
sleeved, the
backpack jarring. over
and over, in a single, insistent murmur:
dwell, had said.
dwell, would
dwell.

THE EARTH AS AIR:
AN ARS POETICA

Tout le mystère est là: établir les iden-
tités secrètes par un deux à deux qui ronge
et use les objets, au nom d'une centrale
pureté.

Mallarmé

for Esther & Gabriel

I

1

lapping of   light over
light,   dew podding the   tall
    ferns   nacreous, as
it
opens (that

~

even here, at
the   very edges it
    start up, this   teasing of
sound out
of

    substance: the
air
paired fibrous
with

    syllables: *moss,   rock, air-*
it-
self-in- syl-

84

lable, that
it

     happen).

~

in twos, that
   it ribbon   forth,   the
      forked idiom's . . . .

each thing
   eithered to   another, the   *this*
   whatevered to the
        that, the
ark-

within-the-
lyre-   propellant: *wind*
and *white roses*

wrapt in a   taut, vibratory weave.

~

because poetry is passage.   is an equipoise-in-motion, addressed
away.

by juxtaposing syllable, word, word-cluster in a harmonious tension,
the poem (both in its materials and its sonorities) channels that
passage: determines its course.

(atomically, by the poem's vibration; discursively, by its dialectic,
its *tao*).

is the body's, first, its profound androgyny's.

fused, inarticulate: insufferable.

that the saying, in releasing, separates: investing each of its opposites, its multifarious twins, with a transparent identity.

that only as 'eviscerates' might they enter the relationship, the *passacaglia*, the poem.

as our breath's oscillating bodies . . . .

is *wind* that permits *white roses* (and inversely).

locked together in their lyric trajectories of attraction, contact, dispersal.

far, what the poem would gather, accord, scatter further.

the earth, in its longing, its shattered fragments —in twos— fluted through.

celebrants in the doom of their invisible transactions, the narrows of their weightless encounters.

that's neither the *enactment of* nor the *symbol for*, but the rites of process by which substance, through sound, is transmitted forth: towards . . . .

the lash-undulant of complements that's

neither the   lily's
nor

the toad's, shem's   nor shaun's, all
our adored decoys of
                              cognition . . .

(what language
 had   seized, set
                         echoing, reflexive,
 through the chambered
 spaces
 of
 our words.

the bounced clowns of   history, one
        the suspended
referent
to the   other: ever, our
                    alien-   commensurates).

            but
            what rushes
            be-

            tween them:
            slips
            be-

            tween
            cabbage
            and

spade, thumb
and
clay in

a gust-
accelerant
of

ashes,
shadows,
of 'things

that are
not.'
neither

earth's
nor
air's, but

the
null
springing,

ebullient,
out
of

a fusion
of
either's. the

nei-
ther's, the
limp,

re-
lapsing
flora of

their
muscles
dulled in

the
wisp, the
wires, the

un-
clemented
rays

shot
from the
hinged

half-
shells: the
echoing

limbs of those
very
lovers.

~

that
it happen!
that the

breath
leap, and
the dark

light
issue be-
tween

our tongue
and
teeth!

in taut banners of shadow, the scrolled motto of the vacuous,
unravelling . . . .

whipped, vibratory.

being nothing in itself: an otherwise-isn't, except for the syllables,
either side, that channel, sluice, project it forth . . . .

there, just *there*, where the syllables touch, join, and in their lyric
reverberations: *release*.

and, so doing, radiate outwards themselves in a sonorous diffu-
sion: an effluvium.

annulled, in successive pairs, by the impact, the discharge, of
their matched percussions.

a 'nothing,' then, propelled by a 'neither.'

a conveyed omission.

the vector of a dark and running silence within the resonant catch-
and-release of every poem.

wedged as we are, as our sounds are, in twos: supplicants, each
time, to that current; that sudden, unsubstantiated breeze.

that soundless bolt in the unwrinkling tin of its quiver.

Being through being (no *Sein* without *seiendes*), as the shadows transit: slip from the intricate cage of their syllables.

radiance of 'sea: moon: pearls: tears,' its compressed immensity.

that it open, break: *irreflexive*.

light's for letting light out.

the poem: for the shelling, the pulping.

'everything I've created has been by elimination' (Mallarmé). 'every acquired truth has come from the loss of an impression that, having glittered, faded, and, in the subsequent release of its shadows, allowed me to penetrate ever further . . .'

to work by elimination implies not a lessening, but a translation of intensities: an *othering*.

as we articulate *away* from ourselves in a continuous elision *towards*.

as the poem comes free of its speaker . . . .

kept, as we are, from entering what we say, from pursuing what we imply, we create a space, each time, from which we're excluded.

the poem is, as such, a quit body: a quittance.

a locution-in-displacement, in ritual flight towards its own reception.

towards that ear, that ether, that *absentia* of all presence: presence itself.

alighting, touching, as it does, upon a separate exhilaration.

and carrying within it, as its null, its no-breath, perhaps the lightest and least palpable of all vapors: that of death itself.

but a death continuously discharged, expelled, projected . . .

a death *kept alive.*

driven from the hoard of our bodies, and cast: oscillated outwards by the syllables themselves: by the play of their tensions, the purity of their releases.

that together, they alight (the 'nothing' and its 'neither,' vector and effluvium) in a luminous tapestry of sound.

the power of its shadows caught —and thus neutralized— within that crossed, inclusive weave.

that depth-conciliative.

neither living nor dead, now, but extravagated, an *ex-vita*, and thriving, twiced, upon the profound surfaces of a second, an alternative space.

as it happens: as the lyric accedes.

through the wind's zero: penetrates.

as the word-errant —at last— touches upon the silence of the word-inceptive.

as if returned, restored to some verdurous, subliminal condition.

in a wash of leaves, waters, songbirds.

aside from the music, inaccessible.

as substance (converted into sound for its passage forth) reverts, at that given depth, to a *still matter*: to the quiescent music of its particles.

in a dimension that we've metrically fashioned, projected past us, and assembled forever *to our own exclusion*.

that substance might transit through us.

unto that grace, that specific perdition, might be received, safe-guarded, preserved in its infinite distillations.

not as our echo or emanation or resonant gloriole but as the exhu-mation of the real, reintegrated.   as the essence of entity itself.

by which all things, unto themselves, are rendered.

by which, by uttering, we *are*.

2

not the
rose for its
damp

im-
pacted odors,
nor

tweezed,
semantic, to
a white

in-
cestuous eye:
our

im-
maculate
mirrors. but

the rose
as votive: for
the

vow
of the rose.
that

washed
in the
cold foam

of its
cratered
petals, is

offered,
boned to
an emp-

ty density
by our
breath.

~

o oceans
in the
heaving

wilder-
ness
of the

un-
cradled
heart, that

the rose be
blown,
spewed,

beached in
the
trans-

parent
salvage of
its

round-
ed
syllable. that

it
weigh, at
last, *one*

with its
absence. as
the rose-

votive is
laid
on the

scalloped,
ray-
blazing

shrine
of the rose-
iconic,

and the two
roses, ac-
corded,

resound.

III

hég   *wud 'ámjedkam*
that-one   is from-thing

it [spirit] is its [signal's] source

from *Piman Shamanism and Staying Sickness*

I

because to stay means to send.

means to maintain this tension, this exclusion, this *physis*; in
residing, to defer.

sending, instead of ourselves, our syllables.

(the breath we'd drawn, still threaded, out of our buried mirrors).

gutted tokens, blown shells!

because it must be given: this space-unsustainable (is, perhaps,
our one imperative).

its words, worked free (from where, still swelling, we'd break:
feed crouching upon our shattered reflections).

but teased —diminishing— into immensity.

to a traced erasure.

to where, inverted, replicated, the two roses, in equivalence,
would touch.

would twice.

the created, at last, syncretic with creation.

sound sounded: plumbed vibratile (shadow and syllable) unto those rippling, mineral tissues.   that 'against-which,' reverberant.

that depth, auroral.

out of which, once, as 'from-things,' the words first devolved.

(while cryptic, within them, hid the roses, the oceans).

that earth be but the dark, sparkling residue of that blown emanation.

our presence *here* but the distance-from.

dense, lexical, deferential.

expelled, as we are, and possessing nothing, finally, but these words, rattles, wind instruments.

these relegating agents of the ruptured air.

for 'in huts, man dwells . . . endowed, godlike, with that most perilous of things: speech.'

that *here* exist, but in the tension; and *there*, in these released syllables posited, deferred.

in space, re-constellated.

over and over, instead of ourselves, *past* ourselves, as if sacrificial.

(the breath, scuttled; the voice, boned).

by which each
thing, unto its   sign-
auspicious, is
rendered:

reeds,
rockfish
and   crystals, the

brief
calices of
the winds-
in-

flower . . . .
(were each
things we'd

seized,
tempered,
held ballasted in
the pressed metal

of
our words (while
their shadows   thickened
off
our breath's

slipped bells).

~

but thinned;
blown, in-

candescent (to where
the words, in
reverting,

would flare . . . .).

by which
wheat
and gypsum,
lightning and
shell . . .

by which
marl,
starling, and
elm.

~

because if we
stop, stop hollowing
substance, and ex-
tracting sound,

stop feeding the
stars
with
their barbed
syllables, then   the
stars, certainly,

shall
have us . . .

                    for
          certainly, there's anger
                    in the un-
          named: in roots and
               pebbles, in   the limp
               rags
                         of   the running air . . .

               is, in each
          word un-
               rendered, the noxious light
               of its   hoarded
                         shadows.

               (for never
          had the heart moved
               through
                         such wilderness; never
               in holding had
               we

               held less).

                              ~

               that the
          either,
                         finally, open   and
               the diptych, in
          its creased whispers,   spread . . . .

               for the sign:
               the
                         sign's trans-
                         parent. the

                              102

earth-worded's a
   station
  in
  space!

      tide-keeps,
        wind-
   keeps, we
stay, that
  each thing, in
    its magnitude, be
         inserted;
   in conjunction,
   set.

  that,
  through us, the
    hazel
might ripen, and   the stars
   into their
      fall quadrants
      drift.

  that, word-

  herded, the
rocks, orchards and
   waves, the

  feathered
   whales, unto
  their twicing, be

acquitted . . . .

~

sorrow, too,
        that in sending we
stay; that   all else transits
            ex-
                cept ourselves.

        are that it   be.
        are that it   thrive: the
sun, in its

            washed
            fires, sal-
            vaged;

            each thing,
            in
            its buoyed scales,
                    as-

                signed.

            'in huts' to
        witness,
        restitute   what is . . . .

        unto
which, as
        offering, this   discourse
                    would rise.

from
VOYAGING PORTRAITS
(1986)

for René Char

saw the glass towers
slip,
    liquid, through the louvered
venetians; the light, in thin
strips, quiver
shut.

. . . .

call: call shapes, faces. . . . each
'heart'
has its
number (its specific
fo-

liations).   even
here, as your

room
rises blanched, amnestic, an
    island, already, in its piled,
pulsate florescence: speak,
ring shimmers.   from
your

sibilants, shake
mass.

~

. . . falls, you'd
say, of
itself,
that
virtue,

                    breath-
tipped, that unbundled
fire . . . .

. . . .

                         here, even
here, contours table, chairs;
runs —in
pinched ripples— to the linen's
slack
re-

lapsing
edges.   (even
here —at this
distance, these late
stations— that script-vestigial . . .).

                    ~

vine, out of
what
voices?   fumes, buds, annunciates of
what
dead injunction?

                              puzzles your
wrist, now, the
tips
of your fingers. . . .   you,
in whom its movement, moment-
          arily, courses: its channeled
pro-
traction . . . .

. . . .

would bring, to the
dark
mouth, its dark
syllables.   being
transitive, 'take, as object,' its
least creases.   into that
re-

cessive, still-indeterminate
image, the fixed
interval's,
enter.

~

. . . .
. . . floated bronze, once, in your
spread
fingers.   fanned damp,
expansive, a ponderous sponge,
in a
dull

shudder of reflections.

            (the projected, at
last, depleted; the image
brought, taut, to that
burning con-
vergence).

~

. . . speak, even
here.   ring
voices.   for the word's
ad-

dressed: a flame
trained to its trellis.   from your
tongue,
now, tease
ash. . . . here, even

here, in this
city

of surfaces (Manhattan gone
violet, glossy, now, in its watery
up-
rights) ex-
tract measure, elicit
sound.

                    '. . . fumes, buds,' but
out of
what
scuttled work?   on which
extinct frequencies, those psalms?
a
breath's

lapping breath, limbs
limbs, that
that ray
shot, into its dark alveole, quaver.

ROAD, ROADSIDES, AND THE DISPARATE
FRAMES OF SEQUENCE

the road, that narrow fiber of running sounds, on which —ineluc-
tably— you'd unravel.

both phrase and paraphrase of your own unbecoming.

(dropped gears; raised ground).

after the cholla and mesquite, the ragged dark triangles of the
piñon.

—were as if fed to those spaces—

to the light's high, dustless, near-lunar intensity.

each pebble, as if pedestaled black.

each object, as if struck, petrified, held —in raised relief— by *fiat*
of some obscure, and now extinct, divinity.

travelled across, a 'transparent slide.'

as if to catch, unawares, your scattered, semi-conscious projec-
tions.

(that dim, disarticulated ore).

"Los Lunas"

—where a water tower, on its tall stilts, quivered silver—

(brief stations of the syllable).

while moving, now, as if past yourself, drawn into ever-increasing degrees of displacement.

so many voices as if thinned, rimmed in static.

edged, inaudible.

(where, through the light chaparral, saw —staring backwards— a pair of hunched, high-shouldered coyotes).

—quills, beer-caps, obsidian—

the very instant the sun, in its ganglion of pink squibbles, went under.

the road, you wrote, began anywhere.

began wherever the words, out of the broken word, first rushed, irrepressible.

. . . the running tape of this sequence.

(wherever you'd finally rid yourself of any notion of return, of personal circuitry).

nights, even faster.

where the whipped ellipsis of lane-markers spun under, and past.

changed altitudes, frequencies, continuously.

(faint, now, the hiss and clipped, metallic snap of *maracas*).

near Albuquerque, neons, printing out palms.

saw (in an all-night diner) your own reflections as if splinter against steel, mirror, tile; burst —radial— to a thin, featureless spray.

as if, even thinner, only the words (the fitted whispers) might withstand fracture.

might wedge —like headlights— a passage.

(creosote in sudden frames through the black, glass-smooth curves).

—might, in some eventual reassemblage, reconstitute image—

what —nebulized— you carried wherever.

night after identical night, through those pink, cellulated rooms, that the mumble might persist.

its tiny, breath-bitten messages be sent, projected past.

(recorded, now, as if forwards).

~

as a dream breaks into its most indissoluble salts.

there, where one by one, cardinal then quail, the still-dark desert awakens.

(already violet, the mocha adobe).

'as a moon seen through the sockets of a puma's skull.'

were journeying, now, invisible to yourself; as if fictive to any eventual other.

—outcrops of red, sun-shredded rocks—

while far out, over them, the quivering mineral of the earliest
mesas.

everything was there, you'd written, except yourself.

dredged air for that vanished anatomy.

(for whatever —once— underwrote 'lymph' and 'gland,' the 'paired
heart of the indivisible').

clouds in thin, driven bands of crumbling nacre.

and, just beyond, on a last, laminal flake of scored sandstone:
Acoma.

(a blush of smoke over its domed ovens).

'eye-dazzler' is the pattern, you're told, on those shattered frag-
ments.

Haako, where resonance, first, determined habitat.

where voice and echo (off its sheer, vertical rock-face) registered
identical.

—the chord, at last, accorded—

of the projections you'd send endlessly past yourself into the end-
lessly emanative: *that transcript.*

(the breath as if gelled in a bell of light).

five hours, now, of penetrated vacancy.   scattered *arroyos.*

now, only so many prepositions with which to fix immensity;
determine, momentarily, a *locus*, an imputable name.

theirs, the 'directional shrines.'

there, where the gold poppies still wind-stiffened in the high chap-
arral.

breath-tooled, those spaces.

from Blanco's on outwards, a taut washboard; a wobbling, dirt
ribbon.

(throb of your blue, wind-shaken sleeves).

'*there*, everything's *there.*'

would press yourself, full length, against the vertical plate of your
own projections.   draw from its deep volutes.

(from each of its gradually unghosted vocables).

as if authenticating, as artifacts, presence and gesture; the very
least ligament, rolled translucent.

Chetro Ketl.

where whole structures, once, were laid out, sidereal.

(a whole world, deferred).

followed, along the facing ledges, that erratic line of calendrical
uprights.

'sun stones,' those squat, chalked-off boulders.

(you between, among them: at the errant center of so much con-
jecture).

pecked steps.

and —as if lacquered black— a high, cloudless sky, overhead.

towards Pueblo Wijiji, intense thirst.

would have drunk, if you could, from your lens' dark, watery reflec-
tions.

(where an eye —scarcely yours— floated over).

charred hearths.

and a random marker, occasionally, to their vanished, ceremonial
roads.

dune and canebreak.

and the sudden, wet stitches of a blue hummingbird.

'later, would abandon these sites, and adopt —like their archaic
predecessors— an itinerant existence.'

with each death, would burn their hovels, move on.

ghost beads, ghost dances.

Kin Ya'a.

there, where the moon floated, diurnal.

later, towards Gallup, saw, in the flowing chrome, your own fea-
tures as if pleat and expand.

. . . hair, forehead, teeth. . . .

(like some small collection of ephemeral keepsakes).

each instant, each object catching, now, in an uninterrupted
sequence of displaced frames.

you, who'd match image with image.

who'd bring the disparate twins —the nomadic— to meet, coin-
cide, superimpose.

—the *you*, at last, within the 'you,' inserted—

(that bundle of wild, unkempt rays).

what, scattered, dissipated, held you, now, in a kind of vacuous
echo, in the ring of a negative radiance.

(while sleeping in the contours of its scuttled volumes).

further south: mesquite, saguaro.

the minute, electrically-charged signatures of the smallest clouds.

only real, seemingly, what you hadn't yet foreseen.

(the idea, at least, that the word, eventually, might possibly pre-
figure).

green slag, and the slow lightning, over.

as the desert breaks now into flat, residential sections.

and the traffic gathers —funnels, five lanes— through the unwaver-
ing rear-view.

117

'tokens,' 'keepsakes.'

or a memory run far enough forward that you might, almost fortu-
itously, encounter some minor, still emergent feature.

(some vestige, projected).

—a sonorous imprint, resilient enough to hold: withhold you—

for the poem you'd compiled and now nearly completed was still
to be written.

still articulated: the length of these relapsing itineraries.

(a syntax equal to all that unhappening).

were so many knuckles, now, studding the black, scalloped steer-
ing wheel.

"(some vestige, projected . . .)"

as the tires hiss —slick— down the damp causeways.

rainy city; shiny palms.

opening, one
after another, our
                    last definitions (way
that the rooms grow, the wrist feeding
on its own words: dark foam,
                                'inexhaustible flower').

---

the tips of the self fill: suffuse but
only towards
                extinction (what the
wrapt mirrors, in their passages, extract).

---

otherwise, of those opaque bodies in
        their moving fields: no
word.   is only the glint that utters (or

                        promises to).

---

you far, even further now
in these vacant
                creations.   through the
        summer's smudged transparency, not even
a teased shadow, slick
                        across a quivering lid. . . .

---

        thrown over and
over onto that hollow heap, the heart
        makes its answers (but
        only as it falls, only

as something light, wasted as itself
                            reverberates).

---

        would wear that cloth, that
exhaustion (the spent
            head of the crystals embedded: en-
        shrined), o bodies beating
                    against their own translucence.

WHAT THE MUSIC WANTS
In Memory of George Oppen

what the music
wants is
pod and tentacle (the thing
wiggling,
wild

as washed
hair, spread).   is our-
selves, in-

serted.   within
our
own rhythms: wrapt, voluted,
that miracle
of
measure-

ascendant.   *to*
stand, that there's some-
where to

stand.   marble
over

moorings, the
scaffolds, now, as if
vanished, and the steps, the
floors: spoken
forth.   *to*
stand, stand there, with-

in
sound alone,
that

miracle!

                          is what the
waters comb, and the
bells,
beating,
count (faint, now, over the

waves, in a
garland
of
bells).   *is*

somewhere, and
wrapt

in the bulb
of its
voices, are buoyant among.

'iodio 131'

1

. . . would wedge this
beneath lids: leave
        messages.   past the last
white orchards, the
winds un-

scaffold. won't
carry our faces, now, like

some
cherished imprint.   'flourish'
and 'wilt' on a
single

semantic branch.   our
manna's, at
last,

begun falling.   hollow steps,
chisel dark.   wrap
your-

self in
the running gauze of this gutted
script.

2

over and
over, but unto

what? no image obdurate, brittle
enough to dispel this
dis-
persion. *sull'Emilia* falls,
keeps

falling, soft onto
wheat, over the
turreted

white
irises and damp,
unplumbed gardens, no
end, no

end to
for-
getting. sprinkles as it falls. . . .

3

washed,
kept

washing. that the hair
stream, and the limbs, through the
strung

gutterals. that
uttered, might
emerge.

~

Ferrara os-
cura.   high, over its
vaulted, oven-
dark
doorways, wobbled gold.   blossomed in

a bowl
of

cupped oils.   no
end, no
light light, measureless enough, but
that our dead
might re-

member.   remember
us.   might eye
the

needle to
these dim fires.   sip,
from our sonorous jars, our verb
tipped, in-

audible.

~

remember, re-
member us that the
heart
both crouch and hover, en-

velop these
shadows in a
foam
of sewn bells.

LINEAGE
for my children

so many voices, there,
vie for the
  voice, crowd sound with the white
pressure of
their

silences.   sea and the tall
rooms, just

over. they're
filling, again, with
mirrors, armchairs, my own as
if

driven enumerations.   the
'moon' there's the
length

of a
line; the 'vase, with
  its ragged, red dahlias,'
                       another.

~

trace.   trace
  forwards.   for only

there, eventually, might issue, might
emerge, not as
entities, but as the
  breath's
very imprint, inflection, the

126

still-
moving rumors of the otherwise
ob-

literated.

      ivory, off-white, nacre: I
read them in
negative. move,
at their restless extremity, forwards.

~

press, they
press me to say: say 'latch,' 'shutter,'
  the 'jade

ladders' the
angled slats make, once

fastened
against the sea. ask
that their silences, finally, be
stilled, muted, the sustained bar of the
un-

expiated,
edged.

~

term,
terminalis. this
  side of

speech, the awnings stiffen; the
charged
barges, running
before the open breakwaters, set
sail.   are

signs, emblems.   are what
there is
as

offering, barter, as the
small, uttered tokens of some momentary
placation.

~

stray
figures.   figments
   of smoke (their muslins,
their
bleached linens wreathed, turbaned in
smoke . . .), we

survive,
survive them, but
scarcely; haul sound, the

tiny
shreds of its
sustenance, forwards.   as if
language
were merely language's edge, its slight,
still-

to-be-
acquitted segment.

                              move, they're
moving, now,
through knuckles, wrists —the

itinerant
sisters, sporadic

brides.   move, they're
moving me to say, say 'jonquil,' 'urchin,'
'kelp.'   to feed them
on
the 'small

saline
scraps of the water's reflections. . . .'
figures
from the far

side (even their bracelets, loose
hoops of
smoke), the

oscillum
quavers.   the air's
curtain

runs taut.   tell them, tell them that the
wind's glowing.   that the
prawns, this
summer, abound.   that now, towards
dusk, the
pines
are billowing from under.   tell them we'd
forgot, that we'd
remembered.   that the

breath, our
breath's vessel, hadn't
rusted.   that, one

by one, the scattered lights of the
low,

offshore islands, the
estuary's, turn
on.

A PORTRAIT OF THE SELF
AS INSTRUMENT
OF ITS SYLLABLES

". . . parmi les matinaux," René Char
As when milk is bound by the juice of the fig, Empedocles

for Robert Duncan

1

. . . was dark,
finally, crossing the Crau, before the
first, blossoming almonds
caught in
the

head-
lights, flickering —pink—
from

under. cupped
flame, that frozen
sequence. (was what
I'd
hold to: the instant-looped, -bezelled,
-set, now,
in-

to sound. the
narrow orchards, now, as
they isle, rise,
the

pos-
sibility, at least, of
iso-

lates).

~

a hissing of
walls,
reeds, wind-
breaks: the running
conjugate

of the
un-
interrupted.

                              (was
what brought me, first, 'a bag, and
briefcase,' the
pos-

sibility, at
least, of stations, intervals, of some-
where where the numbers
might knot, and
the
taut, white boulders, in their

breath-
lines: eddy.

. . . would lie there, the full length
of that
murmur.   'not stillness,' said, 'but the
movement traced, gathered.   the
loose skirts of the
flame in-
folded.   mint

and japonica, brought —quartz-
like— to
focus').

                           a *where*, where-
by the fibers might
run —refluent— into hip,
ankle,
tongue.

within the
circle that, hand-
stamped, cancelled the square: *Lacoste,*
fief of

oak-
smoke and iris.   of
moons

and nettles.   of the black
wind-
pitted cells of
its ramparts (what the
southwinds scooped, and the long
mistrals chiseled).   there, concentric,
at its quarried
heart, where
the

       cobbles
       fork, and the
       hollyhocks

       stand sentinel,
       went

       under.   where the
       lamp
       might root, and
       the

       low
       room glow —bright
       as burst
       straw— brought
       the

broken
swarm of my
syllables, a pulse

beating
against a diaphragm
of

shadows; a
face as
if
poured (so

many
facets) into the
depth-

less mask of its
hands . . . .

. . . .

. . . . that it
take! that sunken,
the

damp
vocable sprout: a
'here'
huddled a-

gainst the
where-

less workings of
a scuttled
earth.   bed,
bottles and chairs:
that

each thing, as it's
uttered,
out of
its

breath.
smoldering, bud!

~

but didn't; wouldn't.   for
ten years, the
rocks wandered.   wouldn't stop: the
shelled meadows, nor the

knuckled trunks of the
stump
sycamores.   drifted Pisces, and Equuleus.
unbound,
un-
threaded, from the
slender wefts
of syntax, floated Sagitta, ashen. . . .
slipped,

what
could trace the weight
of
its own

fingers, bring
the meager echo —its stray body's— to
bear.

for ten
years, reigned
nomen, preponderant.   wouldn't fit, lay
broken, the
phrase in its meted
progressions.   split, severed, what the
verb had
woven (a wave

through its
slack waters
shot, by its troughed rhythms, driven . . .).
a-

drift, now, in so
many
spent components.   in
nomen, the *mundus*
nominalis, each thing, unto itself, in-
vested; each, its
sole
and inflexible referent.   'like

unto like,' the limbs
un-
mixed: that vision Empedoclean, the fusion
of the elements, under
strife, riven.

                    shadows lapping
against chalk, for
ten
years, the
breath went, dis-

membered.   erred bone, erred
measure.   through the *nomen* (in its cell-
ulated
wastes) the poem moved, dis-
assembled, un-
spoken.

. . . . . hung there, a
damp
bulb, a plump
fire, from
under-

neath the
tangled coils
of

her hair.   whorled
taut, each
brittle,
in-

flammated node,
to a
flushed bud, each

knot.   then slack,
re-

lapsing, again, a
loose
effusion, a
heat, run un-

dulant, through
its

rhythmic,
lymph-

rippled grain . . . .
. . . .

~

rung,
am
rung to that that
draws and
in-

volves me; pulls,
cen-
tripetal, from
shank and

tongue. urges its
glowing,
un-
sustainable image
—its im-

print, in
me— through that
narrow draft,
tendon
of

my own
an-

nunciations. brings,
thus, each
word to
resonance, each

breath to
reception. leads
the
least in-

crement into
that
tissue, that
globed air, that be-

gets,

~

. . . brings,
brings, thus, the
poem
for-

wards (of which I
am mere-
ly its
in-

stance: pre-
fix for setting
sub-
stance to

syllable.   for
bringing the
un-
worked images: *damp
bulb, plump*

fire, for-
wards, into their
linked

and sonorous be-
trothals).

~

for the words
wed as
they weave . . . lithe, the
morphemes
couple as the self un-
selves, and sends
its eye moving, deft, through mineral; its
breath, meshed,
through

pine.   mixes
flame,

flour and water; eschews
stasis; abets
rhyme.   binds the
goat's
milk fast to the
fig's
thick juices.

                     'not stillness,' said, 'but
the movement traced, gathered.'   but
sphaïros, the
earth bound, taut, to
its paired
releases.

over Goult, where
lavender foams and lizards —through
the dry
thyme— sizzle,
read
rocks.   read

walls.   saw interstice, manifest.   followed
the low, over-
lapping play of the stones, their ad-
justed
intervals.   past
Les Maquignons, clustered
in its crumbling,
rust-
red ochers, entered
the

trellised air, the wind-
scored

orchards.   (not
cadence, had

said, the fixed
fall
of its
quartered staves, but the wire drawn, the
lines

run rhythmic to
the folds
of the broken ground, pliant to
the earth's
un-

dulant
lay).

                                        not form, then, but
'form as
extension of content.'   but *gestaltung*, each
wave in
its
throe: the
gaudy heave of its

count-
less facets, a
fresh annunciate.

                     ~

                                      nights, would
read, *quouro lis estello
brihon forço*. with-
in the tall,
lime-

washed rooms of that abandoned, dry-
stone cocoonery, read
Blake, read
Char, my

first masters. the
flames rose, in
fat
needles, through the lamps'
glass sleeves. . . . with the least
breeze, the
slack
shadows throbbed. read

144

Sappho and
Pindar, Anacreon

and Catullus.   came
birds, came reeds.   out of
Isaiah, sprang summer; Parmenides, night.
from Dante, that
ore, that
ben

intelleto, and Ibn'
Arabî, those
suspended,
reciprocal

stars.   came
winds, salt, marrows . . . . for the lines, as
they run —transparent— into
dawn, into

light, bring to
each substance its qualities, each
reflection its
light.   proffer their mettle; both
temper and

refine.   came, thus, the
rivers.   came fish, and
the

rain-
shaken lilies.   from the T'ang, thus, the
moons, and the Sung,
mirrors.   from

Mallarmé that
rush

of crushed
shadow, and Shakespeare, that
pearl, its
black

sphericity.   came
thunder, came
tin.   from

Traherne the psalm, burnt
to a glass
whisper.   from Hopkins the
bow, and Wordsworth,
verdurous, the
quiver.

                        . . . for the lines, as
they come, now, un-
written, as they run —pellucid— into
world, infuse, in-
still.   the
syllables fill.   from

Williams, thus, so
many wind-
petaled wildflowers, while from Duncan:
air, that
ayre exultant, and
Oppen, unrelenting, that wheel-

maker's
flame.   from
the

linguists, now (Whorf, Sapir)
how the
least
shift in syntax, tense-
perception, would
re-

set the
heavens; bring a boulder to

tremble in the wrapt
tissues of a
breath.   bring, would
bring us un-

centered, now, onto those very
first
fields: those re-
leased phrases of dust
and dragonflies.   adjunctive, now, to
that

deeper space.   unto that
far

heart, a people, cre-
puscular, who
point.

5

(The Translation of the Waves)

that air not
end, nor
flame
gutter.   that earth not coil —ingested—
into those nounal
hoards, but
verb-

herded, be
given: offered forth.   wind unto
wind, foam
unto *foam*, be pitched, sonorous; through each
meted particle, trans-
mitted.

                              (for certainly to
own is
to interrupt.   to stock, pile, separate matter
from its in-
nate motion —its thrust,
unto— to truncate
and kill).

                    ~

. . . was
what brought me, then, a blue
shadow moving a-
gainst the
glass-

headed light.   a mumble, across the
pruned,
luminous oblongs
of the terraced orchards.   up, over Venasque,
where asters float
to the

fields'
very edges, climbed.
lavender, olive, quince in

laddered
octaves, came at
last to those
waves in
the

rocks.   that
cave

where the waves
hung from
the

poem's
high scaffolds.   *eine*
Pracht —that splendor— *das Werk*
der Wogen.   where, all
morning, they'd
amassed, lay gathered towards their own
trans-

lation.   a-
beyant upon the
brief: *schlägt es*: the
sea, in
Hölderlin's poem, all

morning,
pendant.

                    of the way, the
various ways (angles, torque, tensions) the
waves
might break —fan
against the coastline, foaming— Fédier
and

Beaufret, all
morning, tested
predicates.   Heidegger withdrawn, opaque (a
block of
dark crystal, its
rays

bent in
wards) e-

lucidated the
verb, alone: its clipped, arrested movement.
the back
of his hand
slapped, flatly,
at the dry shadows.

eine Pracht!   all
morning, that
splendor!
that

cave ('no,
certainly
not Plato's') where the
waves in their

great
watery greenhouses ac-
cumulated: a-
waited transition.   in their high, fluttering
aviaries, their
transit.

. . . as
if, in that
vocable, all Europe, all

air —that long morning— were held, suspended.
as if, finally, in the
blue, in-

voluted
wheel of
that

verb-
transfigurant (in *all*
verbs, *all* mornings, finally) the breath would
slip,
accelerating,

towards passage.
wave

unto *wave*; surf bursting
against *shore*; each thing, unto its deep,
im-
bedded mirrors, pro-
jected; unto the running

parallel —its
referent— deferred.
that

thus re-
turned: unto the inviolate, at last, re-
stored, each thing might, in
its turn,
re-

generate.   out of that
lost
language, that buried resonance, might bud:
spring fresh . . . . that
two-

fold, the
earth be —by
breath alone— its
own

recourse.   both
store
and sow, receive and diffuse, articulate its
re-
ciprocal spaces.   that it break,
thus, from that
ul-

timate hypnosis: the ul-
timate Gorgon's
white
monodic gaze.   from its
gases, be

saved.   from that flash and its instantaneous
white fires: *salva, salva*
terram.   was
what the

waves sang.   sang *save, save.*   what the
bells, off the tops
of the
tall waves, beat, flung backwards in
hard tokens, fat
hammered
froth. . . .

~

what brought me, then,
over the low
ledges.   brought that I
bring: impelled that I urge, herd, drive the
words into
that

luminous salvage.   and stand, there, in those
linked shadows, thus
lit.

from
BREATHS' BURIALS
(1994)

for Eliot Weinberger

TRACING A THIRST
for Ed Foster

called it: tracing a
thirst, the poem
as it

sluices a
passage; with each,
dry

utterance, edges
towards its
own

ob-
fuscated source. no,
not the

world, the
world's, but,
per-

haps, its
very
postulate. what the

winds
would lap and the
tongue,

ultimately,
muscle: breath, like
so

many
empty bubbles, brought
to

that pleated lip.

there, once again, at the
   world's
very edge, you're
pointing out palaces, aren't
you? tapping

at that viscous
glass, holding them, the

im-
memorabile, at the
tip

of your
lacquered
nail. there, just there, where the
barge pivots, seems to
station in the
midst

of its own vapors. 'see
it?' you

ask. I see
your lacquered nail, its
wavering
reflection, follow it

across
those stalled waters. *pier, pilaster,*
fronton, the pure scale

of so much
hal-

lucinatory mass. (not even a
hedgerow to break
the

effect, not even
a stray dog, the ragged line of
its
leash).

~

null, in so
many
numbers, isn't this
   what you mean? this, that's
meant? blown
mirrors, the void in

which, turgid, our
viscera

would glow? among the
room,
rooms, the
words empty —spacious— enough to

withhold us? isn't
this, that's
nothing, what the
   cells —wedging— would jam?

~

billows about you, a
scarf of
clouds, pigeons. yes, a sudden
air
of apparent be-

wilderment. tell, tell
me to my-

self, before even
you
get swept
into that wash of sounds, the lagoon,
al-

ready, in a
sputter
of tugs, marked by so

many rigorously
a-
ligned
pilings. yes, before
our own breath hardens
a-

bout its very
words, and our bodies, once again,
beat

against the
muslin of their veiled reflections.

we pretend to be here, don't we?   and sometimes, perhaps, we
really are.   but only drawn, drafted: in the very instant of our
own extrications.

ochre splattered across the facing parapets . . . .

or, occasionally, in the pollenization of certain syllables.

within, that is, the *without.*

the sheer physicality of being alive, but only then: in those buoy-
ant, wind-driven intervals.

the breath —that very instant— giving birth to the lips.

(verb)
what had taken forever, it
seemed, to
reach you, carried you, now, in the
throe
of your own utterance past.

---

bodies without flesh, flesh without bodies: yes, but there, in the
blue cradle of those hollow relocations: the passage.

as the phrase itself as if narrowed to a fresh omission.

coned, elusive.

while each feature in the portrait vanished —seemingly— within
the blind perspective of so much damp, overlapping foliage.

organized as we are about a certain naught.

—an empty ore—

ended, kept ending, wouldn't stop —you wrote— the imminence
of our endings.

———————————

(*either*)

mirror pressed to its
last
unctuous drop, you turn, turn
back, keep wondering
which of
us
will be aureoled, finally, in the other's ash.

———————————

sealed yourself in with signs: with 'lips,' 'forehead,' 'throat;' in a
quarantine of tiny, breath-bitten utterances, subsisted.

for whole months at a time, inhabited a book that would never be
written.

—swarming of silence about the charmed annunciates—

so incredibly far to encounter, finally, those sensuous indemni-
ties: what lay, each time, even further.

———————————

imagined her, her
  entire body as if ventilated by
letter (she who'd
written: "if I await consequence
nothing will

end," ends in passage, your
eyes'
relentless entries).

———————————————

there, in that distant body, your deepest ear.

even now, at the very edge of metaphor, of each earthen compos-
ite, were drawn by the *wasn't* into an indissociable *would*.

dust, dust and petal in the elasticity of inference.

—members tensed—

where from the mesh of so much fluffy, evanescent gauze as if
sipped.

. . . followed yourself
through your own, displaced
worksites (whole
weeks in
the white scaffolds of a single,
   refractory sound). yours, these

arms, organs
a-

waiting conveyance, the
buoyancy of some
exact
syllabication. doves, juniper, the
bright

lime quarries, just over. isn't this
what you'd worked towards? the
world, the world's, the very
magnitude

you'd thin to? wedge,
trans-

parent?

~

                                   whereby the
dahlias, gargantuan, their red petals
un-
dulant as octopi. whereby the
air, the

uttered air, what you'd
bring, in
measured increments, through all
that

dep-
redated space. (*there, in that*
late country, you'd no longer
be
yours. you, who'd

already have reached, by then, the 'may,' the
'might,' the ever-
narrowing
coils

of some tenuous
'could').

is always towards the furthest, and,
   finally, towards the
lost themselves that the senses transit, slip
furtive. that bunched in
muscle, we'd

lusted, it seems, after so
very

little. channels, conduits, the
   secret history —perhaps— of history it-
self, written
in

dark drafts, elusive
scribbles. as if, inadmissible, mass in its
very
densities were
riddled. and you, nothing more

than this breath
that wedged. tongue that
in-

sinuated.

           ~

                oh eyes so pale, you'd
written, they'd
promised grottoes. oh holy, the
grottoes, the hollows, the weird birds of
our own,
dis-

articulated heart. (what, in
de-

fault, had
been plundered,
re-
lentless).

~

                                        'an earth, but else-
where,' isn't this
what you meant? what you'd say? what the
eyes rising —yes, so pale,
    so
impervious— already divulged? for *here*'s
only here in the vocable's
forced

re-
tension. past, past
ourselves, in our own, sonorous dis-

persions, resonates the
gloriole, the
ring

of things released. the rocks, just
⁻now, as if a-
float
in the puddle of their own shadows, and the
papery, pink blossoms of the
cistus, rife

with light, with the very
light, it would

seem, of some ultimate
ac-
quittance.

~

massed, now,
a-
long the edges, awaited —you'd written— no,
not the barge, the puffed
barge, but the

particle. but the
predicate, be-

fitting.

                    yes, holy the grottoes, the
hollows, those excavated worlds which
lie, luminous with

sound, there —just
there— past the inviolable lines of
our own
fore-

closures.

Designed by
Samuel Retsov
and Gustaf Sobin

•

Text: 10 pt Caslon

•

acid-free paper

•

Printed by
McNaughton & Gunn, Inc.